First Facts®

LEARN ABOUT ANIMAL BEHAVIOR

ANIMAL
HIBERNATION

BY JEANIE MEBANE

Consultant:
Bernd Heinrich, PhD
Department of Biology
University of Vermont, Burlington

CAPSTONE PRESS
a capstone imprint

First Facts is published by Capstone Press,
1710 Roe Crest Drive, North Mankato, Minnesota 56003.
www.capstonepub.com

Library of Congress Cataloging-in-Publication Data
Mebane, Jeanie.
Animal hibernation / by Jeanie Mebane.
p. cm. — (First facts. Learn about animal behavior)
Includes bibliographical references and index.
Summary: "Discusses the animal behavior of hibernation"—Provided by publisher.
ISBN 978-1-4296-8266-4 (library binding)
ISBN 978-1-4296-9310-3 (paperback)
ISBN 978-1-62065-255-8 (ebook PDF)
1. Hibernation—Juvenile literature. I. Title.
QL755.M43 2013
591.56'5—dc23   2012002130

Editorial Credits

Christine Peterson, editor; Alison Thiele, designer; Svetlana Zhurkin, media researcher;
Laura Manthe, production specialist

Photo Credits

Alamy: Juniors Bildarchiv, 4, 21, Les Ladbury, 13, Rolf Nussbaumer Photography, 14,
Visual&Written SL, 10; Dreamstime: Karelgallas, cover (inset), back cover, 1; iStockphotos: David
Parsons, 17; Minden Pictures: Ann & Steve Toon, cover, FLPA/Jurgen & Christine Sohns, 7, npl/
Nigel Marven, 18; Newscom: Colin Bogucki Stock Connection Worldwide, 8; Shutterstock: Denis
Dore, 9, Depiano (pattern), throughout, Eliks (background), throughout

Essential content terms are **bold** and are defined at the bottom of the spread where
they first appear.

Printed in the United States of America in North Mankato, Minnesota.
022013   007194R

TABLE OF CONTENTS

When Winter Comes

Cold winds blow. Heavy snow covers the ground. Temperatures drop below freezing. How do some animals survive the winter? They hibernate.

Hibernating animals find warm winter shelters and sleep until spring. During hibernation, an animal's temperature drops. It breathes less often, and its heartbeat slows. It doesn't need to eat or drink much. Many hibernators live off stored body fat until spring.

Which Animals Hibernate?

Animals of all sizes hibernate in winter. Bears are the largest hibernators. Smaller animals, such as woodchucks and chipmunks, sleep through winter too.

Some animals find other ways to survive the cold. Wolves and squirrels can find food and stay warm in winter. Other animals **migrate** to warmer places.

Animal Fact!

Angle wing moths in the Arctic rest for winter under tree bark or in hollow logs.

migrate: to travel from one area to another on a regular basis

In Madagascar, dwarf fat-tailed lemurs can't find food during the long dry season. These lemurs **estivate**. They sleep to survive the dry conditions.

estivate: to spend time in a deep sleep during dry or hot periods

Do Hibernators Eat?

Before hibernating, animals eat and eat. Bears sometimes gain more than 40 pounds (18 kilograms) a week. The extra fat helps them live through winter.

A chipmunk can store up to 8 pounds (3.6 kg) of food in its burrow.

Some animals eat during hibernation. Chipmunks carry berries and seeds to their **burrows** in cheek pouches. They store food in their burrows and wake up every few days to eat.

burrow: a tunnel or hole in the ground made or used by an animal

A Place to Rest

Many animals dig burrows deep below the **frostline** to hibernate. Chipmunks and other ground squirrels dig winter homes with rooms for sleeping and storing food. They hide the entrances under rocks, trees, or bushes.

Black bears and grizzly bears dig dens in hillsides or under logs. They curl up inside with grass, dry leaves, and moss for warmth.

frostline: the deepest point in the ground at which soil freezes

Under Covers

Some animals crawl under things to stay warm. Wood frogs and box turtles crawl under rocks, logs, or piles of leaves. Snails slip under rocks and leaves too. They make hard chalky lids to close their shell openings. Their shells become snug sleeping bags.

Animal Fact! Hibernating slugs cover themselves with layers of slime to help them stay warm.

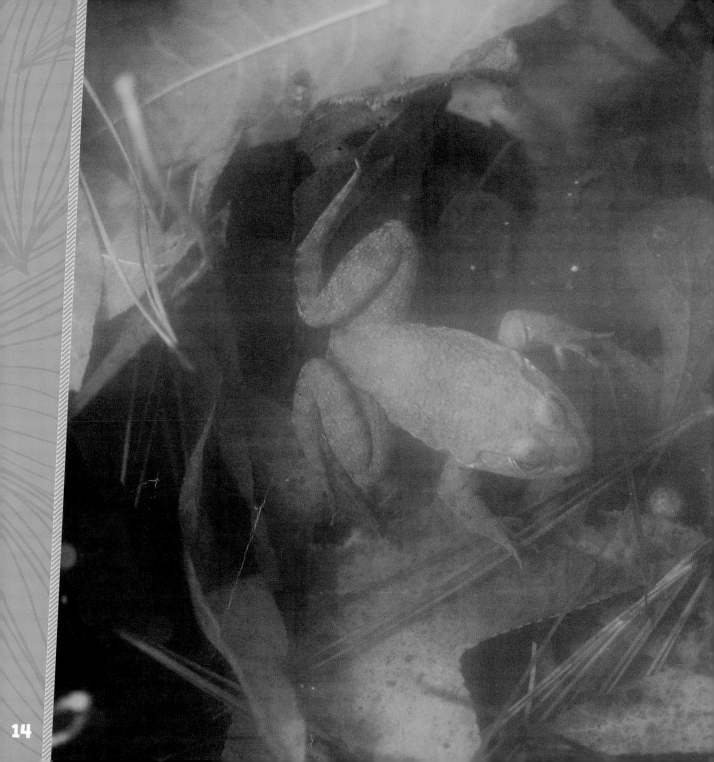

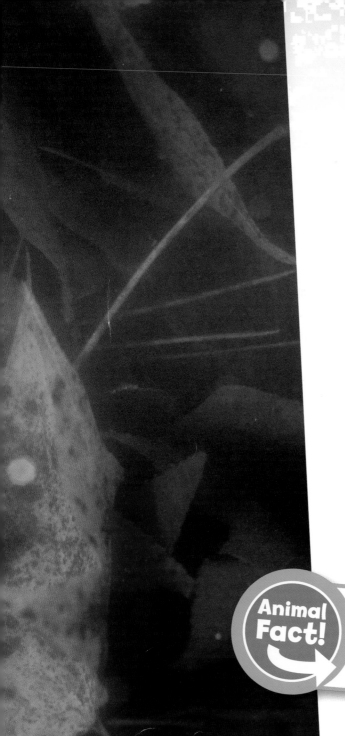

Down in
the Mud

In winter, ponds form thick ice on top. But under that icy roof, animals sleep. Snapping turtles and frogs spend the winter buried in mud on the pond bottom. The mud and pond water keep them from freezing.

Animal Fact!

Wood frogs can partially freeze and survive. They stop breathing and their hearts stop beating. When they warm up in spring, they breathe again and their hearts beat.

In Dark Caves

Bats sleep where it's buggy, damp, and dark. Caves give bats the moisture and warmth they need during hibernation. Bats wake up now and then to drink. Moisture also keeps their wings from drying and cracking.

Animal Fact! Many bats hibernate hanging upside down by their toes.

Alone or With Others

If you could peek at hibernating animals, what would you see? You would see woodchucks and male bears sleeping alone. Hundreds of garter snakes coil together in dens. Small animals, such as female skunks and marmots, hibernate in groups.

Animal Fact! Female bears give birth to cubs during hibernation. Tiny, blind, and helpless, the cubs stay with their mothers until spring.

Waking Up

When the weather gets warmer, hibernating animals **sense** it's time to wake up. They move slowly and **shiver** to help get warm. It takes chipmunks and other small animals nearly an hour to wake up. Larger animals can take several days or weeks to fully wake up.

Animal Fact! It can take bears in cold climates up to three weeks to reach normal heart rates and activity levels.

sense: a way of knowing about your surrounding

shiver: to shake with cold

Amazing but True!

Grizzly bears and American black bears in the Rocky Mountains eat moths before hibernating. These tiny insects help the large bears gain weight. A grizzly can eat up to 40,000 moths per day. Some bears eat enough moths to provide nearly half the fat they need for winter.

Glossary

burrow (BUHR-oh)—a tunnel or hole in the ground made or used by an animal

den (DEN)—a place where a wild animal may live

estivate (ES-tuh-vayt)—to spend time in a deep sleep during dry or hot periods

frostline (FRAWST-lahyn)—the deepest point in the ground at which soil freezes

migrate (MYE-grate)—to travel from one area to another on a regular basis

sense (SENSS)—a way of knowing about your surrounding

shiver (SHIV-ur)—to shake with cold

Read More

Bailer, Darice. *Why Do Bears Hibernate?* Tell Me Why, Tell Me How. New York: Marshall Cavendish Benchmark, 2009.

Lundgren, Julie K. *What Do Critters Do in the Winter?* My Science Library. Vero Beach, Fla.: Rourke Pub., 2012.

Nelson, Robin. *Hibernation.* Discovering Nature's Cycles. Minneapolis: Lerner, 2011.

Internet Sites

FactHound offers a safe, fun way to find Internet sites related to this book. All of the sites on FactHound have been researched by our staff.

Here's all you do:

Visit *www.facthound.com*

Type in this code: 9781429682664

 Check out projects, games and lots more at
www.capstonekids.com

Index